I'M ALLERGIC

I'M ALLERGIC TO PETS

By Maria Nelson

Gareth Stevens
PUBLISHING

Please visit our website, www.garethstevens.com. For a free color catalog of all our high-quality books, call toll free 1-800-542-2595 or fax 1-877-542-2596.

Library of Congress Cataloging-in-Publication Data

Nelson, Maria.

I'm allergic to pets / by Maria Nelson.
   p. cm. — (I'm allergic)
Includes index.
ISBN 978-1-4824-0980-2 (pbk.)
ISBN 978-1-4824-0981-9 (6-pack)
ISBN 978-1-4824-0979-6 (library binding)
1. Pets — Juvenile literature. 2. Allergy — Juvenile literature. I. Nelson, Maria II. Title.
RC585.N45 2014
616.97—d23

Published in 2015 by
Gareth Stevens Publishing
111 East 14th Street, Suite 349
New York, NY 10003

Copyright © 2015 Gareth Stevens Publishing

Designer: Nicholas Domiano
Editor: Kristen Rajczak

Photo credits: Cover, p. 1 Juan Silva/Stockbyte/Getty Images; pp. 3–24 (background texture), 5, 9 iStock/Thinkstock.com; p. 7 Sergey Lavrentev/Shutterstock.com; p. 11 greenland/Shutterstock.com; pp. 13, 15 Alexander Raths/Shutterstock.com; p. 17 Jupiterimages/Thinkstock.com; p. 19 Margaret Miller/Photo Researchers/Getty Images; p. 21 Fuse/Getty Images.

Printed in the United States of America

CPSIA compliance information: Batch #CS15GS: For further information contact Gareth Stevens, New York, New York at 1-800-542-2595.

CONTENTS

Boldface words appear in the glossary.

All in the Family

Does anyone in your family have pet allergies? Allergies are caused by your body **reacting** badly to matter that's commonly safe for most people. People aren't born with pet allergies, but you're more likely to be allergic if a parent is, too.

The Causes

Dogs, cats, **rodents**, and horses are the most common pets people are allergic to. These animals' saliva, or drool, can cause allergic reactions. So can their **urine**. Most often, though, the animals' skin **cells**, called dander, are the problem.

Dander spreads around the house because animals shed, or lose, their fur and hair. It sticks to your clothes and furniture. Pet dander is small and can stay in the air a long time. It's very hard to get rid of.

9

What a Reaction!

Pet allergies can seem a lot like a cold. People with pet allergies sneeze, cough, and get watery eyes. Their nose, mouth, and throat might start to feel itchy. Reactions commonly happen soon after being around pets.

11

Pet allergies are often worst for people with **asthma**. They'll have a hard time breathing. Whether or not you have asthma, if allergic reactions get worse or last for a long time, it's time to see a doctor.

Take the Test

Some people are allergic to many pets. Others are more allergic to dogs, for example. A skin **prick** test shows what's causing your allergies. A small amount of an **allergen** is placed under your skin to see if a reaction occurs.

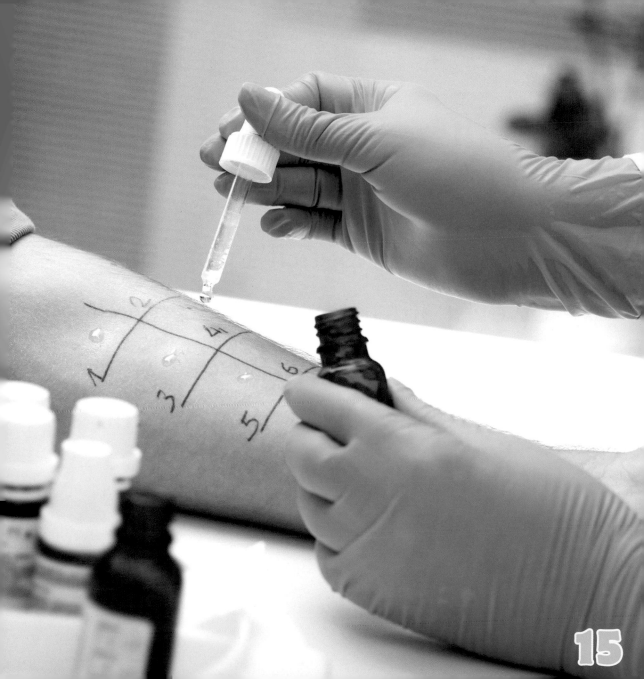

I'm Allergic—Now What?

Will you have to find a new home for your pet? It's possible. However, it takes months for your house to be allergen-free. You won't feel better right away, and you'll be missing your pet! Try some other ideas first.

To keep allergies in check, bathe pets often. Give the person who has the allergies at least one room that pets aren't allowed in, such as their bedroom. People with pet allergies should try not to hug or kiss pets, too.

Staying away from pets is the only sure way you'll have fewer allergic reactions. Some drugs can help, too. Certain kinds of pets are less likely to cause allergic reactions. A lizard or fish could be the right pet for you!

GLOSSARY

allergen: matter that causes an allergy

asthma: an illness in which a person's airways become narrower

cell: the smallest basic part of a living thing

prick: to break the skin with a sharp point

react: to respond

rodent: a small, furry animal with large front teeth, such as a mouse or rat

urine: a yellow liquid containing water and waste products that flows out of an animal's body

FOR MORE INFORMATION

BOOKS

Helmer, Marilyn. *Sharing Snowy*. Custer, WA: Orca Book Publishers, 2008.

Levine, Michelle. *Allergies*. Mankato, MN: Amicus High Interest, 2015.

WEBSITES

All About Allergies
kidshealth.org/parent/medical/allergies/allergy.html#
Read about the many different kinds of allergies and how to live with them.

Pet Allergies
animal.discovery.com/pets/healthy-pets/pet-allergies.htm
Animal Planet's website offers many helpful articles that can help you and your family deal with pet allergies or choose a good pet.

23

INDEX